COMMUNICATIONS

BY

ROBERT ZUFALL

*Our mission is to efficiently provide the world's finest, most comprehensive
book publishing service, enabling every author to experience success.
To find out how to publish your book, your way, and have it available
worldwide, visit us online at www.trafford.com*

Trafford rev. 08/03/2010

 www.trafford.com

North America & international
toll-free: 1 888 232 4444 (USA & Canada)
phone: 250 383 6864 ♦ fax: 812 355 4082

The Road

And now consider gloomily the road,
Following itself, whip-curling, and white lined,
Ended and never ending, down from the holy city
Into the holy sea, going and motionless
Beneath the sky solidified perspective.
Oh, stop your ears, and bind me to the mast!

For each thing is done is done for the last time
And also the first time;
For the first is always the last time
And you will not ever know the answer.
Flat bottomed clouds are piled on a plate of glass.
Someone has drawn a path between the ditches.
We shall not pass this way again.

Contents

Young Love Present

Singing in the green and golden mountains
Soft as the breath of a sweetheart; yet I feel
Laughter, faintly, of old men and of children
Whirling on the swift upswing of life's wheel.

Laughter amid the soft hemlocks in the valley,
(She has seen me and is coming to the door)
Less lovely than her step on the oaken floor.

A wild exulting voice above the ridges
Gives shout, and a thousand echoes, ash and red,
Rush pounding over the stillness, each one joying;
Joying the strong blood surges through my head.

Suddenly the golden door flies open;
In a ruby mist the heart beats on its mate;
And. the singing is a voice I have remembered,
"If you'll let me loose you can have supper. I just ate

And ever the far-off strangely joyous laughter,
Eternally snuggling down in the breast of the night,
Hiding its face in the sheltering wings of the silence,
Wriggling gently away if you hold it tight.

The Washington Express

Neon streaks gash the smooth racing blackness,
Flash from the gutter puddles twisted;
"Bar and Grill" becomes a puddle of fire.

I think I have been that heap
On the sodden doorstep, dreaming
That a woman with big dark hips
Is going through my pockets.

But the broadshouldered rails are perfect in the
moonlight,
Rocking me and the Washington Express
To sleep, standing beside our cradles in the moonlight;
Proud and cosmopolitan they flick
My pal of the doorstep neatly backwards
Into the comforting shroud of the dark.

Poor bastard. Infecting the sterile paper
With my soul's virus, I know as you know,
For you have felt these things, the sleep-breathing
Of the Washington Express,'til it yawns and stretches,
And groans to a stop at New Brunswick.

You have twisted the neon signs
Because they struck at your soul's face swiftly
With bawdy, garish clubs

They have been sluiced away in the laughing torrent
(The stuff that they put in those golden baptismal
fonts);

And we who have shuddered can joy in the sting of the water,
Naked and washed and happy-and unafraid.

The Matador

The juggernaut bull comes straight,
Predictable and fast,
The frightening horns a toothache in the groin,
Intestine, bladder holed.
The straight obese aficionados stand
And wave their hats,
Play suicide, their bravery in me,
Who does not fear the bull.
I think sometimes she wanted me to die.
Here on a velvet is my gift
I give but once
In love and vengefulness.

Ack-Acks And Lawnmowers

<u>The worlds revolve like a country preacher, mowing the
lawn in his naked feet.</u>

The artist is painting with his lawnmower,
Bold encircling strokes till he has gone over
The none too finite green expanse
A couple of times. And then he stands and pants.

Tomorrow (Saturday) he must prepare a sermon
Exhorting extermination of the vermin
Infesting his congregation (arrogance
In farmers who damnwell ought to have more sense).

Grimly he eyes again the mower handle,
Flexes his toes (bare feet, defying scandal),
Spits on his hands, and hitches up his trouser,
Remembering Mrs. Adamson and how his bellow cows
her.

Tomorrow night they'll go to the theater,
He and his wife. Perhaps he won't berate her
If she cries where it's sad. He has felt the restless pain
Of a not quite useless sermon once again.

BLACK TREES

Now as the black trees splinter, groaning,
Ripped by the nations' fire and ice;
Now, as the world's again atoning,
Sullenly paying a usurer's price;

Now, when the tunnel-god looms insistent.
Driving us still to stumble on,
Light at the goal polaris-distant,
Light from the entrance almost gone;

Now I have closed my eyes and found you
Standing before me; your eyes caress,
And they prism the sun iridescent around you-
And I know that the thought of your eyes will bless.

At four in the morning it's dark and the stars are like fire;
The barn is a shadow-form filled with the breathing
cattle;
and the milking begins, for at seven the milk truck goes
through.

Somewhere a red squirrel slips from a snow-laden branch
And. falls swearing to earth.

"So-o Janet. Bill, we'll need feed by tomorrow.
Think old Joe can make it through to the highway?"
"Kinda looks like he'll have to. Start in on Brownie."

Black ice on the millpond booms in the chill, and a
rabbit
Stirs in his shivering sleep.

Oh, holy night,

The milk streams hiss as they cut through the foam in the
pail.
"What time is it gettin' to be?"
"Just a -so-o,   bossy -

Twenty to five."

The stars are brightly shining,

The hemlocks are black against the stars; and a horse
stomps,

A bobcat screams and the windows of the barn are yellow;
The snow crust sparkles where they gleam.

It is the night

"No, Joe, you don't eat 'till you've hauled out the milk cans."
The horse nickers softly.

Of the dear Savior's birth.

Interdependence

Hot rails burrow into a blue haze eternity.
Shining, they strain the eyes as they disappear;
And, learning against the clinging wind, eyes have followed them
Lifting, mirage like, to a steely sky.

The rails are of a bigness with the wind
That clutches at the thighs and curls the dust,
Horizon - bounded: but the measured rails
Have a billion minor atlases beneath.

This is important, that there are such rails, To ride like seagulls on the stolid ties,
Numb and well hardened to pain as the polacks who hammered them,
Interdependence is important, and the trains.

Interdependence, that a billion ties,
Nonentities, wop laborers, should hump
A billion sooty backs so a pounding god
May speed unfathomed souls to an unknown place.

The War Years

I

His weakness was His strength;
But all of us
Drop eyes and hesitate,
Or won't pick up the phone;
Smiling, fuss
Politely at our plate
While dragon's teeth are sown.

II

They say it is neurosis when
A man feels guilty killing men.

III

Our greed is our undoing,
Yours, and mine,
And Rockefeller's,
And John L. Lewis's
And Joe Stalin's.
Without it squirrels wouldn't last the winter.
With it, we may not.

IV

It's hard when first you see it in your own
Kids, your immortality;
Big takes little's candy, or her toy.

It Is Not God

It is not God within me, but a thing
Dirty and warm like a furry mousehole,
A huge loathsome thing like a fat thigh
Onrushing and overpowering. Within
Or somehow near it small precision,
Slime and fertility, the headed sperm,
A completely unacceptable thing
That must be taken, sharklike fish
To which I bare my skin.
Soft cuddly desirable sweet things
Elude me running. The hopeless patient cry
That children, overwhelmed by night
And death and smallness, sobbing cry;
The temple locks our weakening fingers try.

We, Who Would Synthesize A Symphony

We have endeavored to drown, at times in a cup,
The vanity-coring voices that still protest,
"Fool, or not-fool, look within, and sup
A draught of the stark impotence of despair.
Twist your dull eyes inward, let them rest
On your reeking gut-convolutions, that digest
The stricken lamb, and the soft seductive pear,
Transmute their freshness into vomit stuff
That soon is you." And thus your mind, foraging
'round,
Ingests the sun; you find in an hour there
No sun, but a liquid-incoherent guff,
And infant-bewildered sob that the sun is not found.
You, who would synthesize a symphony,
Groping would delineate the sun,
Know that, though your brushes all drip honey,
They will paint only a stomach, and only one.

Maple By Streetlight

Maple by streetlight patterns on the cracked sidewalk
(In your blood is my other world)
Soft and sweet maple smell we go hand in hand having
first lately kissed
(And in my dreaming is your dreaming)
To take soda at the corner drug for every moment is
like the first moment and every soda like
the first soda
(For in your heart is my desiring)
Moths fluttering delighted at the brink of the miracle
shudder fearing the ecstasy of the flame
(And in my soul is your soul a little forever.)

On Beauty

"And what is this 'beauty'?" we asked of the sage
Who sat reading his book by the river's edge;
Reading or dreaming or resting his eyes,
For he was old and tired and wise.

"Beauty", he said, and his voice was slow,
Slow as the river, and lifeless as snow,
"Beauty is not, say, a woman's hair,
But the heart of her lover; the beauty is there."

Silently the river swirls,
Smooth; as the old man's finger knurls
Scrape on his cane, and the pale eyes stare
And his old lungs pull at the evening air.

" For beauty is borne on the hurrying wind,
Borne with the dust to the quick and the blind;
I cannot tell you of what it is made,
Beyond what philosophers have said.

"'The concrete expression of joy abstract, .
The sublimation of human fact' ,
The happiness that the music brings
Is only because you've a heart that sings."

I Must And Cannot Tell You

I must and cannot tell you the word that is everything;
Pebbles strewn, tall grass, and the motion of clouds
    have no importance.
And the shape of building and phrase is meaningless
    and the lights moving in the empty swell of the
    East River.
For none of us knows the whole word but it is
desperately
    important that I try to tell you of it though I am not
    worthy.
There is not counting or touching it but you must know
it;
    you have seen it in a kiss and a handshake and
    through tears.
But God almighty you must know that there is one
word
    that is life and that is meaning and without it
    it's all ash heaps.
And you will know it in the faces you love.

Morning

From the lower level climb to the gray street
Cold in the littered wind, the escalator
An uphill river beside the angled stair.
Car lights pale now with the paling sky
And overcoats stand by a coffee and roll.

In The City

In the city near the river is the sulfur smell,
And the garbage on the quay;
The banana peels are rocking in the greasy swell
Where the sewer empties out into the sea.

Snow

The snow comes horizontally
And up, as much as down;
But, within an hour, see
How thick the blanket's blown.

Successively the piled bits
Transfigure verity,
The crisscross flying crystals hit
And hide us quietly.

The world is not the world tonight,
But is a sculptured place
Where bright soft feathers catch the light
And splash it, in your face.

And we are all alone tonight,
Hidden within the storm,
Deliciously at home tonight.
All primitive and warm.

The Ant

Solomon held the ant to be
A paragon of industry;
And all the ants of Judah's day,
But for their seed, are passed away,
Thriving, industrious, and dull,
A thousand generations full;
And our contemporary ants
Are equally anxious to advance.
Now here's what Solomon didn't tell;
Grasshoppers have survived as well.

You Look Better In A Hat

I used to think that I would grow
To be someone you'd want to know,
Influential, rich and wise,
Wearing discreetly striped ties.
But now that I've many ties to wear
I do not think I so much care
For the feel on my neck of a silk cravat
As I should care for a bowler hat.
Some day maybe when I'm braver
I shall go without a quaver
To a gentlemen's outfitter
Sure that he without a twitter,
Showing a deferential molar
Will be glad to sell a bowler.

See how the Ganges rings our holy city,
Blocked and confined with arduous artifice
So river's river and the city's dry
And the bridges lift above the jostling ice.
The channel must be free, dynamically
And socially, acceptably directed.
The great black molten belly to the sea
Cannot be stopped, but it can be corrected.
When love runs like a river, strong and deep
Small butresses dry swamplands of desire.
There's hardly ever water in the street.
The countryside is hardly ever drier.

The Form Of The Deity

The form of the Deity is nondescript
Here in this darkened room
Since you have lately departed
There is a gray misshapen empty space,

The bright minute of the handclasp disappears
And there remains
Only the contour of the ceiling
        And to sleep.

As aching I watch your shoulders go
And pivot into gone
        I must believe
It cannot be otherwise than this:
This choking thing we have
Impalpable, imperfect, yet the most perfect
Must not die.

This is the measure of eternity
Here, with the shade drawn,
Sleep comes slowly in the sweaty night.
Each parting is a little death
And yet the shining cord sings stronger still
And will, I think
After the last parting.

Jungle

Often times I want to call
Again at your jungle
And have you visit mine.
Unkempt the irritant underbrush.
Wet vines and ugly runners hang
From the thick lacing boughs.
It's muddy underfoot; but once or twice
Fortuitous flowers have sprung,
Great tall and yellow things
Too bright perhaps to live.
And gloomy, but a thread of sun
May lose its way, unknowing catch your face.
But the many rooted banyan is frightening,
And the snakes and voluble birds.
Not many will return,

I have prayed again
While the rain makes its usual black circles
On the usual pavement. Oh, Christ,
If I had any meaning it was to my friend
To whom I said that I believed
That there is much more to love
Than strikes the least casual eye.

Regular Army

You are the uniform, uniformed,
The spit of each the other, row on row,
File, column, rank and echelon,
Like cans of cabbage.

For who would choose a secure slavery,
Goalless, knowing or wanting no distinction,
Nameless. Rank will pay and serial ferret out
Your I. D. card.

But for the one magnesium-bright moment,
Bursting, "Do you want to live forever?"
The shock, not knowing how it came, wet earth,
And you are dead.

You living fail, wither without the will
You fausted for the five year hitch, to drink.
Parade, and drift. What eagle would be hen
For coop and corn?

Between Us Now

Between us now
Goes silence.
The first November snow,
The structure of the heart
Repeat through the length of the world.
For snow can only fall and heart cry out
At the silence between.
Heel and sole cut pavement cookies
From the frail wet sheet.
Though no two flakes, or people,
Exactly match
Variety still is circumscribed,
And methane will be methane
In the silence of Mars.

Be Happy - Go Crazy

When a million commuters to Flatbush and Queens
Throw themselves in the Grand Central Shuttle,
sardines
Had it good; they don't know what it means
To be lost in a river of elbows.

The horde's a conveyor belt, pouring each in
To a bright labeled can like a fruit from a bin;
Can goes bloop; when it's full down a tunnel of din,
And dribbling them out in the suburbs.

Hung on strap like a beef you can look at the signs
Of brassieres that give ladies those high youthful lines,
You can read in your tabloid of horrible crimes,
And the cigarette that makes you happy.

God! It isn't the shoving, the fearing to smother,
It's so many nobodies hating each other;
And nobody's any's acquaintance or brother,
'Till the last zero leaves at Canarsie.

Queens Boulevard

I

Tail lights crawl east in the evening,
Six hesitant red lines.
Gears grind in and out of Egypt;
Daily gapes the Red Sea.

II

Shoulders the holy city in the smoke,
Ground Zero's head triumphant in the sky;
This is the most, the biggest pile of blocks,
The greatest target.

III

Sooted windows light the rusty bed,
Mice rattle between the walls,
Bullets sock the spam cans in the mud,
The Dutchman trims her sails;
And there are a million flying wheels,
A thousand tailpipes.

1 January 1954

It seems fitting, at the orbit's close,
The end that must repeatedly begin,
That this is, more than other days, a day
When feeling of soft blankets in the dark
Signifies rebirth.

I have said
That words must be transparent as the sky,
Shop windows' curved invisibility,
Show heart to eye.

And also said
That words are hammer, chisel that may move
The uncut stone that is birth, death, and love
To shocking brilliance in the sun above.

Breath clouds the glass; and yet I want to give -
(I cannot tell you what you do not know.
In blue-green deep there stings the blinding snow.
Feet, lungs cry out; and goggles will fog over.
Yet buoyant water, lifting wind are rapture.)

The hammer's clay; but I would try to give
(To go alone together from the town
And watch upon the summit, up, and down)
My loneliness, to make your sorrow fade,
And then my fear, to make you unafraid.

Yellow And Black, As A Raincoat

Cleopatra's river is gold in the yellow sun
And trumpets cover us, a thousand horns
The molten brass sings unbearably
Full of forsythia
The heaviness that is past breathing
Too strong to swallow
And words are not words but your trembling lips
The froth of waiting lungs, the cry of birth,
"Hi! Where ya been?"

But on the other hand it was, will be
Not always easy to arise at six
Fear death and insignificance until you
Run to greet them.
The tiller's warped, tonight there is no star
Yet failure is a heavy stone
Plucked, eyeballs in the sand
Strewn for the skeptic's sacrament of suicide.
"Okay. So long."

For The New Golgotha

They say there would have been no time
To fall, or pray, or grab your child,
Turn, run, duck in a doorway.
Free neutrons geometrically
Progressed. We crucified again.
Round flat brownish faces
(How many thousands?) turned
Startled to the flash, and knew
No more. Or, broken by writhing beams,
Awaited the crackling heat. Silent
And wondering (a stolid people). Perhaps
Only the smaller children screamed.

National conscience spreads so thin.
We Christians murdered, while Christ wept.

Horizontal

Inaction is attrition, inanition.
Flat position will condition the volition,
Vitiating all the mating and creating;
Vegetating hating waiting for the crating.

Goldbrick

And you have seen the furtive fearful faces,
Unassuming and incapable,
Ego confusing psyche and physique,
Evolving backache.

Princeton Revisited

Lightless, lifeless, colorless pearl gray
Above the flags, wet concrete tiers beneath.
The raccoons and chrysanthemums are wet.
Atavistic, chauvinistic, proud,
Loving conflict, too well bred to fight,
Too old, too weak, too lethargic to play,
We drink and shout acceptable expressions,
Inaudible to those who wear the cleats,
(So sharing in communion of the school.)
And afterwards we're awkward at the club,
A little tight, and tired, and out of place.
Home is full of strangers, so we leave.

Restlessly moving and endlessly steering directing,
The slow pitch and roll and the ceaselessly changing
direction;
Break off! I would go to you now,
Now, swiftly, in dark, on the empty streets.
Within me the seed has split open, I feel the roots
searching,
I would stand in perpetual amazement at your door
Out of breath from running say over and over, "Hello-"
Finding you sleepy in the streetlight I would hope
To lose myself. To lose myself,dissolve-
Or that we frozen might twine our roots
A hundred years together standing firm
To contemplate the beauty of the world.

1=1,000,000

One identifies with one;
And who can feel
The anguish of a many zeroed number?

A thousand lighted doorways
Are a village, from a plane.
A thousand deaths, ungraspable,
Become as less than one,

The one I have felt within me several years.
The great ship circles for a bobbing form.
One mourns the death of millions;
And millions mourn a pope.

Speed Laws Vindictively Enforced

No crossing solid line
No parking anytime
Bridge may be slippery
Keep left for parkway

No stopping on the grass
Right at next overpass
Autos yield right of way
(Arrow) TP NJ

Speed Limit 45
Southbound E. River Drive
Squeeze left 1000 feet
Gas-oil-dine-Eat.

October

It is not the falling of leaves, that is not it,
Too much repeated, occasioning less note
Than harlot starlet's loves, or ads
For cigarettes. Drying the supper dishes
With dark at kitchen windows waiting outside,
Emptying garbage, hauling the dead ashes,
Throwing coal; it's often closer now:
How many Octobers, and how little done;
How many more before the setting sun?

Call Quietly Goodbye

As you go, call quietly goodbye,
That, sitting, I may know
(Dreading loneliness) you go.
Run slipping along the gravel,
I shall not see the place,
Birdless, where propellers sing,
Slapping at the dust.
In the cold sunrise, go

Looking At Houses

Shapes move quietly in the stillness
And the old house hovers
Malignant with the shapes of death
And aged illness.
A letter from a crumbled lover
Thrown and swept
Seeks copulation with old bottles
In the dust.

I grow older but I do not grow more wise.
Escape is troublesome at best.
Small monuments are left; some songs may rise.
The poor worm cannot rest.
This insecurity is an abyss,
An altophobia.

House patterns endlessly repeat
And group like ants about a sweet.
All day we walk on bones

Patient In Time

Patient in time we have lain together
And pushed with our toes at the sand,
Patient and warm as a snake on a rock,
The sun like a hovering brand.

Not waiting in time for a thing that would happen,
Ingnoring the introvert eye,
Like a bear under rocks in the snow heavy woods,
Or a hawk leaning shoulders on sky,

Suspended in time and the sun and the water,
The world-long rush of the sea;
I kicked at your sand-sticky jellyfish foot,
And was pleased at its proximity.

My Last Duke

The red leaf lilts and arches
To yellow pool below,
Delicately lurches
Spiraling and slow.
Smoothly circles widen
Reflected from the shore
And fade in small confusion,
A fugue without a score.

My dear, the fall has early come,
The sunlight fades so fast.
Sue, bring the tea. Ah, please have some,
Now that you're here at last.
I'm glad you came. It hasn't been
But seven years or so.
You haven't changed; but have you seen
How younger others grow?
But let us sit here on the lawn,
This wrought iron chair for you,
Until the evening chill comes on
And covers us with dew.
You like the pool? I thought you would.
We'll have to drain it soon.
The young folks, yes, it does them good,
To splash the afternoon.
See how the lawn slopes past it, to

The boxwood hedge behind.
George loved that hedge. But what of you?
You know, you're very kind

To leave your home, to fly out here,
To stay with us awhile.
Not many childhood friends, my dear
Would even write. I'd smile
But when he called my name in there,
Just one short, frightened cry;
I found him lying by his chair,
Where he'd stood up to die.

No sailing then, or even tears.
I held his body fast,
And prayed, and thought how many years;
But Nature's cruel at last.
For life needs death to feed upon;
And one gets bored with things.
I wish he lived; but now he's gone,
And reading solace brings.

I saw no soul, as he grew chill,
Wing saucerlike above;
And if there wasn't any, still
We'd thirty years of love.
But here's our Susan with the tea
And cookies. Thank you, Sue.

We got your favorite kind, you see,
And now, one lump or two?
For I believe God loves us all;
He'll square us up all right.
Ah, but forgive my funeral pall,
I'll spoil your appetite.

Monday Morning

Forever rose fades slowly under the bell glass,
Is, and is dying; forever dust films the polished table.
The filled grain flexes, strains the satin glaze,
Sketching the rose. Sweetheart, I must go;
The tower is lighted, they are waiting in the glare.
The anesthetist has placed his mask. They are sweeping
the streets.

Afraid

We have been always afraid, and sought out danger
Since fear and excitement are one
And there is an instinct for anxiety,
A wish to be afraid,
Braced on a sharp-edged rock, to feel the wind
That cuts with an icy knife across our faces.

Ski Tracks

It's like being a deer,
Almost not touching the snow,
Leaping down endless slopes
Of endless whiteness.

We Who Walk

And we who walk between the windowed walls
And stare at square and glare, the towered halls,
Where even grace is tension, coldly feel
The straight unrecognizability of steel.

Things of the crumbling earth are earth. Forlorn,
We must return to what we did not form;
Make pilgrimage with fishing pole in hand
To find again a hatrack in the sand.

BUM

I did not ask you, help an old man out,
Or would not ask, but these three kids, these guys,
These dirty hoodlums; I had forty cents.
The El post rivets cold against my face,
Cold are those iron buttons. I can find;
I had a room, a gray harsh woman there,
She cooked for me, I lying in the bed
Or at the window, counting rivet heads.
Or lying beside them, people going by;
I was not drunk, but still I couldn't more.
I can find; but then I couldn't find
The rows of dirty doorknobs, lodging house.
They lock you out at six, or if you're drunk.
I may have hated once. The rumbling trains
Come round about me. I got folks down south.
So then these kids - I think my arm is broke -
And dirt falls on you when the trains go by.
She threw me out. I think my foot is froze.
The dirty bitch. You gotta help me out.

The Garden

Workers in stone make permanence,
Shaping wet concrete.
A hot forenoon has endurance
Past the summer heat.

Sweat spots mark the boulders,
Laying up a wall.
You and I grow older;
The rocks don't change at all.

The moment of congealing
(Lava at Pompeii)
For centuries revealing
What we made today

Supple nasturtiums blow away
Or wither in the cold;
Yielding petunias troop their gay
Colors before they fold.

Diggers in dirt, givers of birth,
Pressors of seed to ground,
Dampeners of arid earth,
Gardeners abound.

The vigor's in the secret seed,
The reproductive cell.
The cosmos carelessly will breed
Certainly and well.

Serenade

Thus our affection rebounds
Like the toes we pressed together
When we sat idly watching
Water's idle motion.
See, it has lived through much forgetting.
The times, the places blur,
The record beneath a deepening stack
Of memories is filed.
Affectionate sounds we made
Have ceased to stir the air.
The motion of the water is the same,
Forgotten parts are dead and fallen off.
Let us say hunger for love
Is greater than thirst after knowledge,
And when I have wholly forgotten you
I will have died.

Out Of My Heart

Out of my heart flows ceaselessly thru tubes,
That tumble underground, a fluid chant,
A kind of metered song, a reverence
That, blind as a compass needle, gropes its way
In plunges down the hidden artery.

And so turns smoothly, as a torso turns,
With light familiar motion of the arms,
A fluid force less measurable than blood,
A chemical reaction that proceeds,
An aspiration to eternity.

And equally, as leaves and robins turn
And worlds, and tufted titmice to the south
I turn to seek you out, to come and sit
Beside you, in the magic of yourself;
Receive the benediction of your love.

Grandma
1875-1959

Old, old, old,
The mystery
Is older than wreaths.
You are here.
The corpse is not
The personality,
Unlike the magician's card
You will not reappear.
Temporal boundaries
Are drawn,
Matter is only changed,
The snow you brushed from my snowsuit,
Macaroni and cheese, after milking, yellow light
On the night shining snow.
The candle is caught in the wind
And no one asks
Where did the fire go?

Lamps

The lamps become black against the windows,
Then the windows behind the lamps
Of this great unoiled machine,
This wrinkled earth
Whose every crack is castastrophic.
We have all existed for two billion years
And I recall
Some several times of vivid happiness.
And after that the earth was beautiful,
Beautiful, beautiful world.
A small boy rubs his stomach on the grass
And I can look at you.

Ride On Water

Ride on water
Afloat like the ancient's world
Olympus a turtle's back
Culture's cradle rocking in the sea
Afloat with endless cancelling motions to move
Not to arrive today but only feel
The changing pressure on your hips and feet
Seeking the bottom level like a swing.
Only avoid
The gust that breaks the balance,
Lee gunwale under, and the hissing brown
Snakes that swirl suddenly, the boat, surprised.
Staggers and falls, old gouty cripple,
Drowns.

Pause Here

Pause here for reflection,
Hands on the rusted rail;
Steer out of direction,
 Hang like a windless sail.
Angling sunlight dimming,
Peace is a time like this.
See the brown trout swimming
To stay still, where he is.

The Parthenon's Columns Are Curved

The columns bend a little. Curves are rich;
Unstable equilibria obtain.
Learn to walk carefully, avoid the ditch
For sin is indiscretion, I explain.

Arching toward each other, slender necks
Incline in decorous gossip, delicate
As flames sucked in a spiraling vortex,
Drawn by the currents they themselves create.

Geometry is straight, and Empire State
But not the sounding brassness of a bell;
And stresses curve and calculus and hate
And boomerangs. And love returns as well.

Virus

Slow to a fumbling crawl, be overcome
With lassitude, succumb to gravity
And ennui. The liver, bowels and throat
Pinned by a cunning pain, the wires slack.

Daybreak

A day shatters into many fragments,
Shiny, sharp, and bright,
Out of the weakness of awakening,
And into the funnel of night.

In A Quiet House The Sound Is Startling

In a quiet house the sound is startling,
Wave on a rock
And then ablution
Making a vortex down
The funnel whence all excrement is sent.
Evil so late within me is cast off.
The dross is gone.
The better part remains.

Magnificence Needs Squalor

Magnificence needs squalor;
The granite grandeur, rock on polished rock,
The cables of the many-leveled bridge
Jump from the island where
Small bilingual dirty shirted boys
Play stickball in the street.

The Pale Impartial Sun

The pale impartial sun
Arises late, half heartedly.
The leaves repeat the turning of the world,
Flare like the agonal flare of a meteor
And curl in chromatic convulsions as they fall.

The Age Of Restlessness

This is the age of restlessness.
Clambering down around us
Discontent seeps into seams
And pockets of accumstomed jeans.

We repeat the unlearned movements
And the learned tritenesses
While a desperate ache burns deeply.
Fire hollows a rotten tree.

Discontent

Discontent seeks meanings.
Lying gratified in bed
Or after a thick steak and baked potatoes
There are no meanings; have you found it so?

It is not so much a fear of death;
But I shall hate to go
From love and laughter
So little known, or said.

Can I tell you how I saw him bleed
The naked guts outbulging from the wound
Feeling the cold whispering of wings
Knowing that some do not grow old to die.

And not at the moment of death can be insight,
The eyeballs dry, the losing fight to breathe;
Consciousness is lost before the end,
A gurgle for the parting bon voyage.

When all the splashes have gone the water is quiet.
The spray returns greening into the far depths
Suggesting wisdom. Caught and analyzed
Only, and amazingly, water.

We will proceed identically, meaning or none,
Bound by the logic of the chromosome
To eat, protect ourselves, and reproduce
Hoping that fate is not fortuitous.

Perfection

Perfection is immobility, a scale.
The brazen weight is weightless, quivering.
In palpable potentiality the pans
Strain at the polished arm.

And so we talk,
Poised and immobile as the table top,
In words that hang within a dustless case.
In trembling innuendos we imply
Ecstatic chaos

And a broken scale.
Perfection is a tightrope walker, dear,
Toes twisted on his taut security.
To sin is to encounter the abyss
At either side.

A poem's a thing
Composed for a loved one to read; and in that sense
A poem of love, a movement toward immobility.
Yet love is the only dynamic. We balance or fall.

Rocket Goes

Rocket goes
Cloud blows
Tree grows
Man sows
Fish glows
Iron flows.

Rat
Brother rat
Be kind to
Web footed
Enemy tribes
Girls walk
Alternate rounded calves
Even acquaintance
Mitigates
Must be destroyed
To save the world
Old buddy

Look Down

Drop clean and neatly,
Hang on a sliding edge;
Slip past the rime-squat trees,
Spiral down through white
And the numbing wind.

Rest where the hemlock boughs
Drop silent snowballs;
Below, a breaking treetop
Scatters shards of ice.

Then rock and balance,
Kick a fluffy spray;
Fly down the crested side
Of the mountain.

Solar Cell

Sometimes I feel
Like a solar cell
Subsisting on unstable
Sunlight,
Easily uncharged,
And always forgetting
Forgetting;
Juggling chunks of
Irredeemable time
And changing shirts;
Forgetting until
Only caresses remain
And the shadow of sunlight.

Big Wet Flakes Come Slowly

Big wet flakes come slowly
Like the days
That whiten my head.
The struggle shifts
Slowly to survival from success.

Snowflakes

Who would offend a snowflake, kill the snow?
Soft things that change the frozen earth and go
Still softening, and almost I am free,
Almost believing, almost in ecstasy.

Fire

If I could paint I'd like to paint a fire
And hold on a canvas its endlessly changing perfection.
The flickering flames are like raindrops that fall in a puddle
Recalling hypnotic the face of half buried desire.
Look at faces of friends that have turned in the fire's direction
And see that they see the thing too, in the flickering subtle
Designs that are disappearing and always the same.

Being exactly what it is, a fire
Because it can be no other, achieves a perfection
Dancing like raindrops, steaming the snow to a puddle
Leaping to life on a log like a bright new desire;
And the old disappointments are bearable, there is direction.
We know, I suppose, that the fire is our brother. The subtle
Remembering embers are lonely and warm and the same.

Word

A word is a bell
Hung from a rock
(Or easy dust)
Significant sound
Call children up
Or angels down
And going does not know
Its reach and echo

Now Find Again

Now find again, the trumpet cries,
Now turn again to find inside
Reverberating heart there lies
The baby who was crucified.

The columns rise beyond our sight
That hold the heavens in their place,
And coruscating clouds of light
Obscure benevolence's face.

The sound that catches fire within
Awakes the shimmering harp of joy,
And boughs that bend with snow begin
Obeisance to the baby boy.

That Blackness Folds

That blackness folds fast over and around,
The headlights push it out it wraps behind
The two red tail lights and the license plate,
 For you and car and black are still, the road
A piece of space and time that rolls beneath.
You could be anywhere: the half read sign,
Aurora or the gates of hell, some miles.

Posture Of Penitence

Ominous is the time of martydom,
Posture of penitence, abiding time,
Frightened of motion, or the lack of it,
Afraid of the guilt within the sexual urge,

An unspent rocket fallen back to earth,
Scattering fire in meaningless gyrations
Of unguided impulse, a compass that swings
To every magnet, never pointing North.

There's loss of manhood in the bended knee,
Fearing removal may have been accomplished
Or desired, excision of the reproductive seed,
Granting immaculate sterility.

There's guilt for parricide, the infant arm
That strikes, and then, in terror of the switch,
Goes up again to pray. We who know hate
Know that we must have punishment for peace.

Slower

I tire more easily, and get through fewer books.
Heaven can't be a big glass bottomed boat,
A subscription to Eternal Time magazine
Of happenings we cannot influence.
Will we exist not as matter,
Nowhere in the knowable
Nestled at the un-feet of the Lord?

Hide From The Sun

Go hide from the sun.
Shrug off his long straight fingers.
Run from his slow, constant march.
Press to the wall, and he will finally
Catch you full in his red eye
And slowly grind you up and spit you out.
Go hide from the sun.

Perfume on concrete
Issues from the door,
Or secret apertures
Of Lord and Taylor
(God and clothier);
And little trees in
Great square wooden boxes
Prove that the ancient
Elements are here
Though much disguised.
It warms the chill
Damp smog and hints
Of fluffy pillows and of
Thick piled rugs.

Soft Where The Brown

Soft where the brown has faded into white,
Watching while appearing without sight,
As secret youth lasciviously might,
I watch you, bending, make the embers bright.
Your legs stick a little together. Yellow light
Of night will find your hips, define delight.
There is no greater ecstasy than this;
To watching know your presence in the night.

At The Bar

It is easier to say to you than to myself
And easiest in this dark peopled place
Across this table, in this paneled room,
Most serious matters are, I should suppose.
I am a coward. All we drunkards are.
A student of bars-authority, perhaps.
No, you don't see pink elephants, though I
Have had hallucinations. No, I don't
Remember much about them. Memory fades.
I know I was frightened of something, something strange.
Anxiety must take those fearful shapes.
You know the smell of paraldehyde? It stinks.
I wonder if the DT's are a fear
That you had when you started to drink. A fear of death.
Policemen, and great curving sharks, and bugs
All threatening death, of course, for some old sin.
And you crawl in the bottle again when you hear them
coming
Dissolving in the whiskey till you're gone.
They cannot find you. Dirty-mouthed pistols, too,
And a straight line projected forever are more frightening
Than a floating corpse or paraplegic snake.

Ungirdled Memory

To tempt ungirdled memory:
Cold potatoes and gravy,
The pouring from a spout of tea.

Stair treads with the brown paint scuffed,
Castered legs, and pillows puffed,
Pluck at the chair, pull out a tuft.

Dust and rust on a music stand,
Asphalt shingles in serrated band,
Knees of knickers wet with sand.

David

His round unwrinkled eyes
Think vaguely for themselves
Stare equally at me and at the lamp
And do not know.
Recall I think, less womb
Than you, anesthetized, recall the knife.
Bottle directed, a creature of oral awareness.
And yet some bottles later
In his bed
The eyes converge on mother
And he smiles.

Corporate complacency compiles
The Annual Report. Your Company
Is happy to relate that even while
The world, the country, and the industry
By pressure and adjustments were beset,
Still your management has minimized
Adverse effects and bravely ended up
200 million dollars in the red.
Under competition we've achieved
Increasing cash flow and economies.
Explored new areas that, we believe,
Mean future growth and mysteries
Toward which we, lances set, will carry on;
That glow is not the sunset; it's the dawn!

Ignore Strangers

Now, after some years, I sometimes
Can ignore strangers
Seated next to us,
Or standing in a line -
Not entirely, but
As you'd ingore a tree
(And not in mens rooms, where
I'm still afraid.)
I don't try to love them anymore,
(Children of God,
46 chromosomes,
Intraspecific attraction,
Unbelievably
Complex machinery,
The hang of their jackets,
Good old sex)
Since it seems to make no difference to them.

Golf

Awhile we march across obedient grass
Civilized and ringed with planted trees,
Balance above a ball, and follow it
Where in random responsiveness it leads.

Let us step bravely forward on the course
And place our tees with hopeful genuflection,
Resolve to waste our time in verdant scenes,
Forget our hopes to change the world's direction.

Perfect

Skin is the perfect texture,
The pleasantest to touch;
And body is the perfect shape,
Always delightful to watch;
Voice is the ideal instrument
That no violin can match;
Human is the beautiful scent
Perfumers endeavor to catch;
The taste of your sweet lips only
A person could love so much.

Play

When I push you on the swing
I hold you, then I let you go,
Speeding down and up and slow
And backward thru the wind again.

Digging in a pile of sand
We make roads and tunnels,
Houses, parking lots and dams
With our hands and shovels.

To climb upon the great big rock
Rough and scary and round
You need a helper to push you up
And to catch you sliding down.

The tractor tires are fat and black
The trucks are green and red
The bulldozers are yellow
And push the dirt ahead.

Accept

Accept the kind subconscious act that puts
The football fumbled, numbers added wrong,
The bottle dropped and the promotion missed
Into some uncleared closet with a door
Where they sleep and fester and on rainy nights
And chilly mornings groan and thump about.

Bedroom

Shall I tell God that headlights
Arc across the ceiling of my room,
If He exists, that ghostly squares
Sweep unseeing through my furniture,
Or should care, that they make me afraid?

Anthill

At daybreak in the anthill do they blow
Reveille, or do they simply stretch
And shivering bend to lift their grains of sand?

Night Driving In The Country

As in the comfortable sorrow
Of an old bereavement,
Windows, like fireflies at dusk,
Suggesting joy,
Heated and cushioned and bound
To diurnal feelings,
The world disappears
In the sadness of oncoming night.

Buildings, like men, should sleep.
It seems to me
Horrible that all night eating spots must go
From light to brightness, constantly awake,
Never to know the re-creative dark,
Never to find at dawn a cleaner world.

Alone in the silence together, nodding stare
Down the hypnotic highway, passing lights
Significant only to designate the road
(Rooted in rubber, easily erased).

Herb

Oh, the airline crews, the captains and "stews"
See many an awesome sight;
But the strangest one, when all is done,
Came on that fateful flight
When the captain tried with fearful pride
To break his way in the john
And exposed to the view of the folks and crew
Herb with his undies on.
He tried, though the sign said "occupied"
To batter down the door;
And with a shout he called, "Come out!"
But no one answered his roar.
Then he took a key, with stealth and glee
And flung the portal wide.
To see him seated inside.
Oh, what dismay was theirs that day
To see Herb seated inside.
They gaped and stared, for Herb was bared;
And Herb said, "Close the door!"
I like it here, but I greatly fear
That you'll let the riff-raff in
And they'll see me in my BVD's
And that's an indictable sin!"
They shrank away ashamed that day
Of the horrid thing they'd done.
And Herb's returned, his modesty spurned.
To avenge himself for this wrong.

Projector

Flat hills and valleys, cells stained red and blue,
The colored shadow skitters on the screen,
A weightless ghost, not anything that you
Would find with eyes: the fibroblasts are seen
Encroaching, and the neoplastic glands
Insinuate their tiny feet into
The bundled nerves. "Of course this finding brands
It carcinoma, spreading as they do."
This bit of us before us mummified,
This faded paisley glimmers from its glass,
Our little precious tissues dignified
Into vast islands and peninsulas.
Here in the darkness we have grown to be
Upon a wall an abstract tapestry.

The Fire

We stare into the fire, the hungry flames
Licking the blackening logs, and talk of love
And life and happiness and passing time.

First the stricken lascivious match, the flare
That ate into the paper's thoughtful words,
Then caught, if it was lucky, on the logs
And merrily caressed us with its warmth.
Now the orange embers jump and play
With a gray bit of smoke, a dropping ash,
The fire departing, as it has to do,
Or else burn up the house, and then the world.

Not so are love and life, though like a fire.
You showed me that there is a God
To Whom we'll someday at the end return.
I knew already, though you helped me know
That love, if it be true love, cannot die.

I love you in depth. An awkward phrase,
The digging of a well, through nights and days,
Down through the things that any stranger sees,
Your welcome face, your hands, your feet, your knees,
Your dignity. Past what a cocktail friend
Would find, your bright and educated mind,
Through you the colleague or the client knows,
Innovator, whose dedication shows,
Deeper, the mother of our family,
Loved by the children whom she brought to be,
Past layers of mornings, weekends, evening meals,
Until we've told each other how we feel
About so many issues and events
And shared so many thoughts and arguments,
Till I find at the bottom of the well
A clear reflection, somehow, of myself,
And I in you and you in me, since first
We became water for each other's thirst.

To Kay 10-10-1984

I wake you on your birthday with a kiss,
And think how years ago we chose each other,
And think there's no more happiness than this,
A loving family, with you the mother.

For our love sustains us through our lives,
Together in the evening of our day;
My comfort and support, the best of wives,
At work, at making children, and at play.

Today

Today the sun did not come up
As it usually does, fearsome and comforting,
Peach colored clouds, and then the orange spot
You see but cannot watch.
Today wet nourishing rain.
I can't play tennis or ski,
Make love or even write
Or doctor much,
But still somehow life's fun.
There's love, and family and friends,
A little work, and pleasant memories
(Though some of things done foolishly, or wrong),
But mostly happiness to talk to Kay,
And feel the great joy of our mutual love.

2-23-06

To Max

"Come listen while we play for you a thing,
An early work. You'll see in each device
How much one owes the other." So the strings
Tremble with small ecstatic skilful cries
That follow faster, weaving, patterning
A sense too delicate to call a thought,
Gone as it happens, while the fiddles sing.